D0256772

You can Save The Planet

Written by Jacquie Wines
Illustrated by Sarah Horne
Edited by Philippa Wingate
Designed by Zoe Quayle
Production by Joanne Rooke

With thanks to Peter Littlewood from the
Young People's Trust for the Environment,
and Liz Scoggins.

You can Save The Planet

First published in Great Britain in 2007 by Buster Books,
an imprint of Michael O'Mara Books Limited,
9 Lion Yard, Tremadoc Road, London SW4 7NQ

Copyright © Buster Books 2007

All rights reserved. No part of this publication may be reproduced, stored in a retrieval
system, or transmitted by any means, without the prior permission in writing of the
publisher, nor be otherwise circulated in any form of binding or cover other than that in
which it is published and without a similar condition including this condition being
imposed on the subsequent purchaser.

A CIP catalogue record for this book is available from the
British Library.

ISBN: 978-1-905158-78-5

2 4 6 8 10 9 7 5 3

www.mombooks.com/busterbooks

Printed and bound in England by Clays Ltd, St Ives plc

**The book is printed on paper that is certified by the Forest Stewardship
Council. The printer holds FSC chain of custody SGS−COC−2061.**

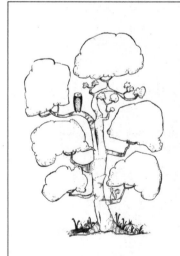

In many forests around the world,
logging still contributes to habitat
destruction, water pollution, and the
displacement of indigenous peoples.

This book is printed on paper made
from trees that are grown in
sustainable forests. This means that
new trees are planted every year to
provide wood for the paper.

Our printer has made sure that all the
paper used to make this book comes
from a responsibly managed forest.

Contents

For every copy of this book sold a donation will be
made to the Young People's Trust for the Environment.
It is a charity which aims to encourage young people's
understanding of the environment and the need for sustainability.

You can visit their website at www.yptenc.org.uk

Help!

Human beings have damaged or destroyed a third of the Earth's natural wealth – its wildlife, its forests, its rivers and its seas. However, the most serious impact of our actions is on climate change. Scientists overwhelmingly agree that the Earth is getting warmer, and they believe that human activity is making temperatures rise more quickly than they might otherwise.

Climate change is probably the most serious, long-term threat our planet is facing. The evidence of it is all around us. The sea ice in the Arctic has shrunk by more than a million square kilometres (386,000 square miles); all over the globe glaciers are melting; the ten hottest years on record have all occurred since 1991; and sea levels are rising which increases the likelihood of flooding and death.

On the following pages you will see evidence of the damage that climate change is causing throughout the world.

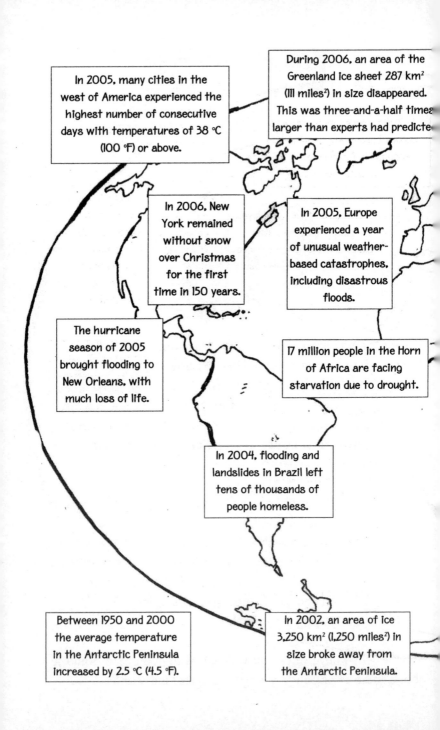

In 2005, many cities in the west of America experienced the highest number of consecutive days with temperatures of 38 °C (100 °F) or above.

During 2006, an area of the Greenland ice sheet 287 km² (111 miles²) in size disappeared. This was three-and-a-half times larger than experts had predicted.

In 2006, New York remained without snow over Christmas for the first time in 150 years.

In 2005, Europe experienced a year of unusual weather-based catastrophes, including disastrous floods.

The hurricane season of 2005 brought flooding to New Orleans, with much loss of life.

17 million people in the Horn of Africa are facing starvation due to drought.

In 2004, flooding and landslides in Brazil left tens of thousands of people homeless.

Between 1950 and 2000 the average temperature in the Antarctic Peninsula increased by 2.5 °C (4.5 °F).

In 2002, an area of ice 3,250 km² (1,250 miles²) in size broke away from the Antarctic Peninsula.

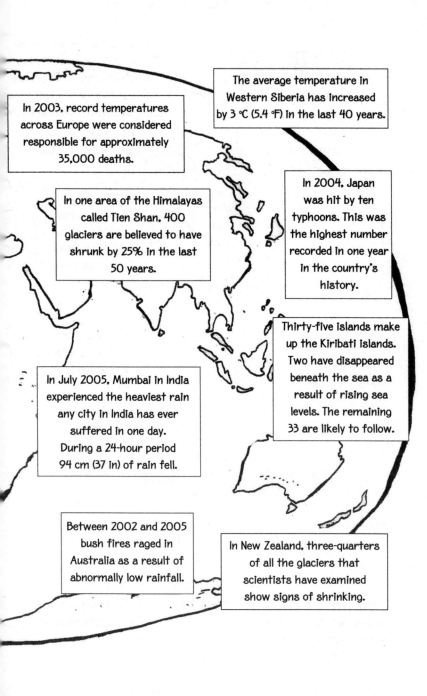

The average temperature in Western Siberia has increased by 3 °C (5.4 °F) in the last 40 years.

In 2003, record temperatures across Europe were considered responsible for approximately 35,000 deaths.

In one area of the Himalayas called Tien Shan, 400 glaciers are believed to have shrunk by 25% in the last 50 years.

In 2004, Japan was hit by ten typhoons. This was the highest number recorded in one year in the country's history.

Thirty-five islands make up the Kiribati Islands. Two have disappeared beneath the sea as a result of rising sea levels. The remaining 33 are likely to follow.

In July 2005, Mumbai in India experienced the heaviest rain any city in India has ever suffered in one day. During a 24-hour period 94 cm (37 in) of rain fell.

Between 2002 and 2005 bush fires raged in Australia as a result of abnormally low rainfall.

In New Zealand, three-quarters of all the glaciers that scientists have examined show signs of shrinking.

In addition to the extreme weather conditions that bring drought and hurricanes, the increasing temperatures are causing the vast sheets of ice that cover the poles to melt. The Greenland ice sheet is the size of Europe and is melting faster than scientists anticipated. If it were to melt completely, sea levels around the world would rise 6.2 m (23.6 ft) and most of Earth's coastal cities could be destroyed.

Climate change is threatening polar bears with starvation by shortening their hunting season, according to a study by scientists.

This damage to the planet is happening because the planet's resources are being used up – in other words, we are being too greedy and too wasteful. We buy vast quantities of unwanted things. We bury billions of tonnes of rubbish in holes in the ground. We pump enormous amounts of dangerous gases into the atmosphere, and we pour sewage and toxic chemicals into the seas and oceans.

Some scientists say that if we don't act now to reduce climate change, in ten years time it will be too late to save the planet. So it's up to you to act. *You* need to take responsibility for the planet's future. Look at the way you and your family live, and make changes that will ensure your household is 'greener' and more friendly to the environment.

In this book you will find 101 simple but effective things you can do to reduce the damage being done to the planet. This book will help you to make the right changes and the right choices.

The Earth's future . . . your future . . . is in your hands. Go to work.

Chapter One

Do You Live In A Green House?

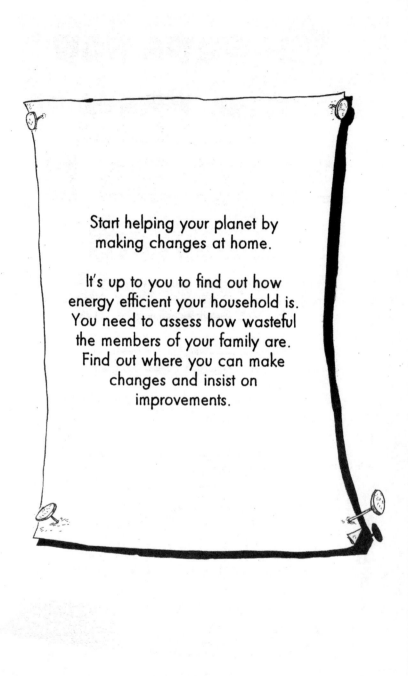

Start helping your planet by
making changes at home.

It's up to you to find out how
energy efficient your household is.
You need to assess how wasteful
the members of your family are.
Find out where you can make
changes and insist on
improvements.

No.1 : Assess Your Excesses

Find out how many energy crimes are being committed in your household every day. Make a note of the following:

ENERGY DIARY

• I have taken a look and our attic is/is not insulated.

• I tested each window in our house for drafts by holding a feather in front of it and seeing whether it fluttered. .... windows had drafts.

• We have .... light bulbs in this house. .... of them are energy efficient, fluorescent bulbs.

• I walked around the house and .... lights had been left on in rooms that were not being used.

• When I checked, ... electrical appliances in the house were on standby.

• The heating/air conditioning was set to .... , but unfortunately .... windows were open.

• I checked the washing machine and the dishwasher when they were last used and they were full/ half full.

.... taps in the house were dripping.

No.2: Switch It Off

Did you know that a colour TV left on standby can use 85% of the energy it uses when it is actually on? A video recorder left on standby uses almost as much electricity as when it is playing a tape.

Every gadget in your house that is left on standby wastes energy. You can often tell if an appliance is on standby because you'll see a little red light on it glowing. Many appliances go to standby if you use a remote control to switch them off. You might not think a little red light can do much harm, but it is costing millions of pounds in wasted energy.

OVER TO YOU

• Check every appliance in your house, including TVs, computers, mobile-phone chargers, DVDs and video players. When an appliance is not being used it should be switched off at the socket on the wall or unplugged completely. Tell your parents they could save up to 13% off their electricity bill by doing this simple thing. They will be saving money as well as saving the planet.

15

No.3: Choose The Right Light

Check out every light and lamp in your house. How many of them have energy-efficient light bulbs?

Compact fluorescent, spiral light bulbs last ten times longer than standard incandescent light bulbs and use 66% less energy. Point this out to anybody who buys another box of 'old-fashioned' energy-wasting light bulbs, and rant at anyone who leaves on lights that are not needed. They'll soon get the message.

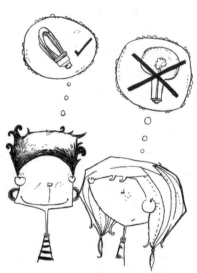

No.4: Don't Be A Fan Of Fans

The next time that you see someone who is cooking reach to switch on the extractor fan above the stove – stop them. Open the kitchen window instead, and tell them this is a 100% energy-saving solution.

No.5: Washday Decisions

Turning on the washing machine just to wash your jeans or a football shirt wastes water and electricity. And did you know that all the detergents you use pollute the water system?

Copy out this list of rules for your household and make washday a more eco-friendly occasion:

WASHDAY RULES

• If clothes aren't really dirty we will use a cooler wash. This saves electricity, because 90% of the energy used by a washing machine is used in heating the water.

• We will only switch on the washing machine when it is completely full.

• We will wash single items by hand.

• We will use environmentally-friendly washing powders.

• We will use less washing powder and we will NOT use fabric softeners.

• We will go easy on stain removers.

• We will try to keep our clothes cleaner so we can wear them for longer without washing them.

No.6: Get Out The Rubber Gloves

An eco-warrior's life is never easy. Sometimes you will need to weigh up the pros and cons of an issue in order to make a sensible choice. Take dishwashers: there are times when it makes eco-sense to turn them off, and times to use them.

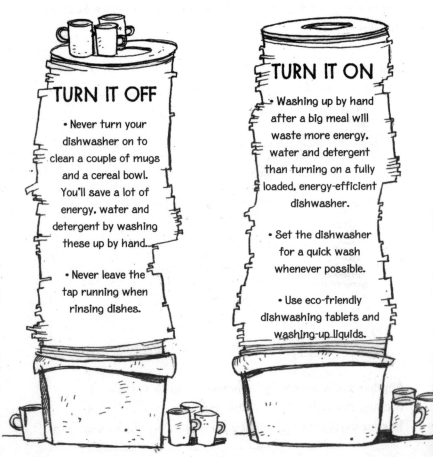

TURN IT OFF

• Never turn your dishwasher on to clean a couple of mugs and a cereal bowl. You'll save a lot of energy, water and detergent by washing these up by hand.

• Never leave the tap running when rinsing dishes.

TURN IT ON

• Washing up by hand after a big meal will waste more energy, water and detergent than turning on a fully loaded, energy-efficient dishwasher.

• Set the dishwasher for a quick wash whenever possible.

• Use eco-friendly dishwashing tablets and washing-up liquids.

No.7: Check That Thermostat

Lowering the temperature on the thermostat of your heating and air-conditioning units by only 1.5°C (3°F) can reduce the greenhouse gases your household produces by up to a tonne. So take a look at the thermostat and check whether you really need the air conditioning that cold or the heating that hot.

Find out about greenhouse gases and the effect they are having on our planet on the next page.

Durrrr!

If the thermostat for your heating or air conditioning is near a window, make sure the window is shut. Otherwise the thermostat will have the wrong impression of the temperature in the house.

Another really simple but effective thing to do is dust or vacuum the surfaces of all the radiators in your house. This increases their efficiency by improving the flow of heat.

Greenhouse Gases

Greenhouse gases are a group of gases that scientists believe are affecting the climate of our planet.

The main greenhouse gases are water vapour, carbon dioxide (CO_2), methane, and ozone. Many greenhouse gases occur naturally, some are man-made, but all are increased by burning fuels such as coal and oil. Burning rain forests also releases millions of tonnes of greenhouse gases into the air every year.

GREENHOUSE GAS

1. Greenhouse gases form a layer above the surface of the Earth, like a blanket. The more gases that are produced, the thicker the blanket becomes.

The Greenhouse Effect

The rise in temperature that the Earth experiences as a result of the build-up of the greenhouse gases is called the greenhouse effect. The greenhouse effect is illustrated below. Greenhouse gases form a layer in the atmosphere above the Earth's surface. This layer acts like a blanket and traps the heat from the Sun. Without these gases, the sun's energy would escape back into space. Instead, the temperature of the planet increases. The more gases that build up, the greater the effect will be.

THE GREENHOUSE EFFECT

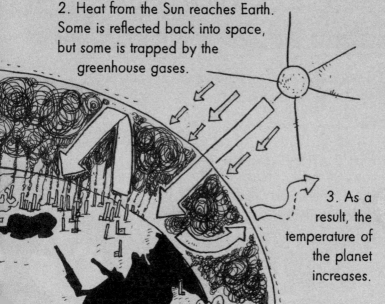

2. Heat from the Sun reaches Earth. Some is reflected back into space, but some is trapped by the greenhouse gases.

3. As a result, the temperature of the planet increases.

No.8: It's Cool To Hang Out

Household appliances that give off heat, such as a tumble-dryer, use lots of electricity. So whenever the weather is warm, persuade the members of your family to hang the washing outside on a line to dry, or arrange the clothes on a rack indoors. Turning off the tumble-dryer is a 100% energy-saving solution.

No.9: It's A Wind-Up

Why not look out for wind-up versions of household gadgets? They make perfect eco-gifts.

You'll find wind-up torches, radios and mobile-phone chargers. There's no need for mains electricity or batteries, all you have to do is wind and wind and wind and wind . . .

No. 10: We Love Layers

Have you ever noticed anyone in your house opening windows while the heating is on full blast? If you spy such scandalous, energy-wasting behaviour going on, take action.

Alternatively, have you spotted someone wearing a T-shirt turning up the heating? Tell the guilty party to put on some layers if they are feeling cold — it's 100% greener.

No. 11: Heat It Up And Cool It Down

This project is probably better left as theory rather than put into practice, because it involves painting your house and your parents won't love that. The colour of your house, and especially the roof, can affect how your home heats up and cools down because light colours reflect sunlight, and dark colours absorb it.

If you want to warm it up in winter, paint your house black. In the summer, to cool it down a bit, paint it white again.

If your parents demand proof of this science working before you paint the entire house, perform the following experiment. On a hot, sunny day, grab two cardboard boxes, some white paint, some black paint and two thermometers. Paint one box black and one box white. Put a thermometer inside each of the boxes, and place the boxes in the Sun. Leave for a period of time and then read the thermometers. The air temperature inside the black box should be higher than the temperature in the white box.

No.12: Stinky Solutions

If your bedroom gets a bit smelly sometimes, don't be tempted to spray air freshener around. A great deal of energy is required to manufacture these products, and some aerosols contain substances that are harmful to the environment. Why not just open the window and let the whole world breathe more easily?

No. 13: Don't Waste Water

Without water there would be no life on Earth. Every plant, animal and insect needs water. Even though 70% of the Earth's surface is covered with water, only 2.5% is fresh water we can drink. Much of this fresh water isn't easy for us to reach, as it is frozen in glaciers and ice caps, or buried underground. So we need to start saving every drop of the drinking water in our taps right now.

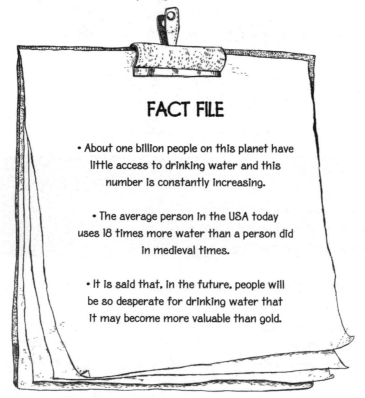

FACT FILE

• About one billion people on this planet have little access to drinking water and this number is constantly increasing.

• The average person in the USA today uses 18 times more water than a person did in medieval times.

• It is said that, in the future, people will be so desperate for drinking water that it may become more valuable than gold.

OVER TO YOU

• Never leave taps running. Up to 7.5 litres (1 gallon) of water can run out of a tap in one minute. Wash your hands in a basin of water, not under a running tap.
Turning off a tap while you clean your teeth will save up to 14 litres (two gallons) of water.

• Nag your parents to repair any dripping taps.

• Don't flush the loo when you have just had a pee. Did you know an average family of four people can flush 375 litres (100 gallons) of water down the loo every day? Write this out and hang it by the loo:

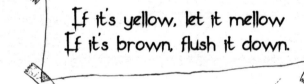

If it's yellow, let it mellow
If it's brown, flush it down.

If you catch anyone flushing the toilet when they have just thrown a tissue in it, tell them off.

• Having a short shower uses a third of the water used taking a bath.

No.14: Don't Poison The Planet

Less and less of the planet's water is safe to drink without chemical treatment because we have polluted it with oil spills, sewage, industrial waste and fertilisers. Don't let your household add to water pollution. Stop anyone who pours substances like oil, paint or cleaning fluids into drains, sinks or toilets. The taste of up to 3.7 million litres (1 million gallons) of drinking water can be ruined by 3.7 litres (1 gallon) of used oil.

No.15: Make Your Own Detergent

Keeping a house clean can make the planet dirty. Polishes, disinfectants, window-cleaning products and kitchen and bathroom cleansers pollute the environment. Just throwing away the empty containers of these products increases the amount of rubbish in landfill sites.

Why not use vinegar and baking soda to clean the bathtub, sinks and kitchen surfaces? Dip the sponge in vinegar and wipe. Use the baking soda to scour the surface clean. Rinse the surface with clean water. Try mixing equal amounts of water and vinegar and use it to clean windows.

Chapter Two
The Great Green Outdoors

Whether you have plants growing in window boxes or in pots on a balcony, or a garden at home, or an area at your school where there are plants and trees, you need to check how eco-friendly the gardeners around you are. Do they really have green fingers? Or do they waste water, and kill weeds and pests with poisons that pollute the planet?

Make sure the plants and wildlife that live around you have a chemical-free environment in which to thrive.

No.16: Watering The Plants

Did you know that the amount of water we have on Earth has always been the same? In other words, there is no more water available now than there was when dinosaurs were around; it simply gets recycled by nature over and over again. As there is no way of getting new water, we need to conserve the supply we have.

In the developed world many people waste water. Make sure your family is not guilty of this.

OVER TO YOU

• Stop anyone you see using a hose to water plants. A hose uses huge amounts of water. Use a watering can instead.

• Leave out buckets to catch rainwater and use these to water your plants. If you have a garden, perhaps you could persuade your family to buy a big water butt to collect water.

• Choose plants for your window boxes, pots or garden that like dry conditions, if that's what you have in your area. Why not plant some lavender or sage?

ECO-BLUNDER

Here's a story that demonstrates how careful governments must be with water strategy.

The Aral Sea, in Kazakhstan, Central Asia, was once the fourth largest lake in the world. However, in the 1960s the local government decided it would be a good idea to change local prairie land into cotton fields. To do this they needed lots of water, so they built canals to divert two rivers that had previously flowed into the Aral Sea.

The lake's water began to dry up and became very salty. The fish in it died so the local fishermen could no longer earn a living. The wind blew the salt on to the land so crops could not grow. Although the government had tried to make things better, their actions made the situation very much worse.

No.17: Plant A Tree

Planet Earth once had many more trees than it has today. Humans have cut down them down in order to make room for towns and cities and to create fields in which to grow food. Today, forests are disappearing fast. Clearing forests and burning trees is one of the major causes of greenhouse gases in the atmosphere. Here are some shocking facts:

THE TRUTH ABOUT TREES

• Every year more than 900 million trees are cut down to provide raw materials for American paper and pulp mills.

• 1,000 million trees are made into disposable nappies each year.

• Every year, 80,000 km² (31,000 miles²) of forest land disappears throughout the world.

• Thirty-three football-pitch-sized areas of forest are being cut down every second.

So does it really matter that all these trees are disappearing? Yes. The main reason that trees are so important to the planet is that they help us breathe. They clean the air by soaking up poisonous gases like carbon monoxide, sulphur dioxide, and nitrogen dioxide. One tree can filter up to 27 kg (60 lb) of pollutants from the air each year.

Furthermore, trees give off the oxygen that we need to breathe. One mature tree can provide enough oxygen for a family of four to breathe for a whole year.

Did you know that trees are the longest living organism in the world, and can grow for hundreds of years?

Yes, but with pollution increasing at the rate it is, trees planted in cities are often surviving for fewer than ten years.

OVER TO YOU

• Get planting. To choose which species, look at the trees in your area, as some may grow better than others.
Get permission to plant a tree at school, in a local park or in a garden. Why not start by planting apple or tomato pips in a pot?

• Don't forget to recycle paper, too (see page 83).

No.18: Why Pesticides Are A Pest

There are some insects and animals we think of as a nuisance because they carry diseases or destroy food crops. So we kill them with dangerous chemicals called pesticides.

In the 1940s, scientists thought that using pesticides would increase harvests all over the world and thereby save millions of people from starvation. In part this has been true. However, most pesticides don't only kill pests. Many have been spread by the wind, or have got into water supplies where they upset the natural balance of the environment.

SOME FOOD FOR THOUGHT

• Only about 2% of pesticide sprayed from the air actually lands on the crop it was intended for.

• Some pests have become resistant to pesticides anyway. These critters are known as 'superpests'.

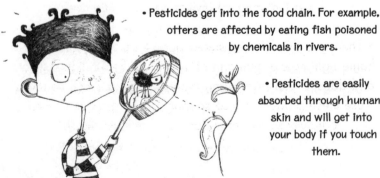

• Pesticides get into the food chain. For example, otters are affected by eating fish poisoned by chemicals in rivers.

• Pesticides are easily absorbed through human skin and will get into your body if you touch them.

OVER TO YOU

- Research greener ways to deal with pests. For example, aphids can be sprayed with water. Weeds can be pulled up by hand instead of killed with chemicals. How about giving the slugs that bother your plants a saucer of beer? Often they will get drunk and stay away. Put the saucer by the plants you most want to protect. Alternatively, surround plants with crushed eggshells so slugs can't get to them.

- Don't use insect sprays. Put screens on your windows and doors to keep flies, moths and bugs out of the house.

- Instead of putting down poison to kill vermin, block up holes that may be inviting to mice and rats.

- There are 50,000 registered pesticides. Many are in your home right now in the form of mothballs, flea collars for cats and dogs, insect sprays and plant-care products. If you must use these products do so sparingly, and dispose of them carefully so that they don't contaminate the soil.

No. 19: Grow Your Own

It is seriously good fun to grow food yourself and it ensures zero pesticides are involved in getting good food on your plate.

How about growing some delicious cherry tomatoes? You don't need a garden to plant them in, just some pots on a sunny windowsill.

The best time of year to plant tomatoes is towards the end of April when winter is over.

1. Scoop some seeds out of a cherry tomato you are given for lunch. Rinse the seeds in water and leave them to dry.

2. Fill empty yogurt pots with some compost. Push a tomato seed into the centre of each pot just below the surface of the compost and cover it. Water the compost lightly.

3. Label your pots clearly (so no one throws them away by mistake!) and leave them on a sunny windowsill. Check them every day, watering as needed so that the compost always feels moist when you touch it. However, be careful not to

overwater them. After about a week you should see tiny shoots appear.

4. After about four weeks, the shoots will have grown into tiny plants. Lift them out of the pots gently, taking as many roots as possible and being careful not to damage them. Transfer the shoots to large flowerpots full of seed compost, gently firming them into position.

5. Keep checking and watering your tomato plants (by this time you may need to water them twice a day). After a few weeks, you should see some flowers appearing. These flowers will eventually fall off leaving tiny green tomatoes.

6. When your tomatoes are bright red and feel slightly squashy, they are ripe and ready to pick and eat.

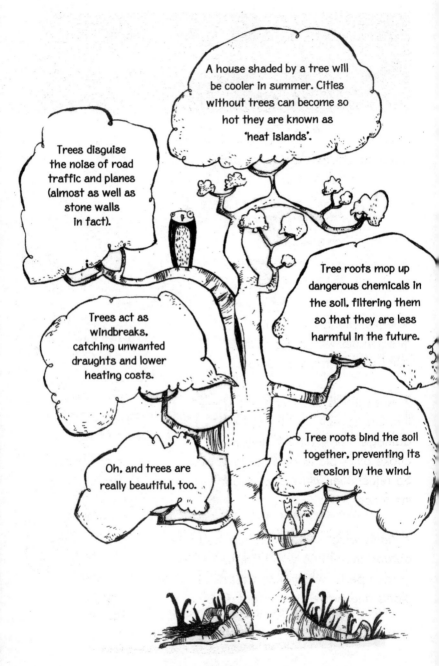

No.20: Be A Careful Planter

Don't choose a plant just because it looks nice. There are more important things to consider.

OVER TO YOU

• Choose plants that provide food and shelter for local wildlife.

• Reject plants that would threaten the well-being of the other plants growing nearby.

• Alien plants are non-native species that can spread rapidly and do damage. For example, they might choke other plants or block waterways. So reject alien plants that might 'jump the fence'.

• Plants which have been imported from abroad may bring with them hitchhiking garden pests, which may destroy native plants and prove hard to get rid of.

No.21: Dig A Pond

A pond was once a feature of every village and farm, but as our lifestyles have changed the number of ponds has declined. This has left many pond dwellers with no place to call home. Many amphibians, such as frogs, toads and newts, are now in decline.

Why not persuade your parents or your school that they need a pond?

1. Choose a site that is level, sunny, and away from overhanging trees. Mark out the shape of your pond with canes and string.
2. Make the edges very shallow so plants can grow there, and animals can get in and out. The deepest part of your pond should be about 75 cm (2.5 ft), so pond dwellers can survive if the surface freezes over in winter.
3. Line the pond with newspapers, cardboard or an old carpet. Overlay this with a sheet of plastic. Then add more newspapers and then soil.
4. Fill the pond slowly to avoid a mud bath.
5. Avoid introducing goldfish to your pond, as they will eat other pond inhabitants – choose some sticklebacks instead.
6. Add plants to your pond to oxygenate the water and provide shelter for pond visitors.
7. Watch as frogs, snails and birds enjoy a new home.

No.22: Another Burning Issue

Every eco-warrior needs to know their ecological facts. If you are going to insist on changes in your family's habits, you need to be able to argue your case and justify your demands.

Unfortunately, some eco-arguments are not clear-cut. There may be reasons for and against a particular course of action. Take bonfires, for example. Here are some reasons for and against burning the rubbish your household and garden produces.

AGAINST

• Burning rubbish releases polluting chemicals and gases.
• Ash can contain dangerous metals, such as cadmium and mercury.
• Smouldering garden waste releases horrid things into the air, particularly when it's damp.

FOR

• Less rubbish in landfill sites.
• The rubbish doesn't have to be transported to dump sites.
• The leftover ash can be used to fertilise plants.

OVER TO YOU

Here are some alternatives to burning waste:

• Why not avoid these tricky arguments and recycle as much of the rubbish your household and garden produces as you possibly can? Find out about all the household materials you can recycle in chapter three.

• Rather than burning your kitchen and garden waste, force your family to compost it.

• Never burn certain items such as fridges, old mattresses, car batteries and tins of paint, as they will release toxic fumes. Always take things like this to your local rubbish and recycling centre.

• Never burn old tyres – try using them to make a swing or to build an obstacle course. Maybe you could use them as plant containers.

• Never let anyone in your family be careless with matches or light an unsupervised fire. Thousands of acres of forest are unintentionally destroyed every year because of fires.

No.23: How Green Is Your Mower?

Here's a shocker – a petrol mower running for a year can produce the same amount of pollution as 40 cars on the road for a year.

Another huge problem with garden mowers is accidental fuel spills. Did you know that if all the fuel spilled when people refill their mowers was put together in one pool it would cause as much damage as a slick from an oil tanker disaster?

So if you have a lovely lawn and the time comes to cut it, make sure your family buys an electric mower . . . or better still a mechanical one – go on, get pushing for your planet!

No.24: Adopt A Hedge

In the UK alone, 322,000 km (200,000 miles) of hedgerows have been destroyed over the past 60 years – that's enough to stretch all the way around the globe. Often, hedges are cut down by farmers who want to use modern machinery in bigger fields.

Sadly, disappearing hedgerows are seriously bad news for hedge-dwelling animals and birds, who are being made homeless and hungry. Some animals, such as foxes and badgers, use hedges as 'roadways' for getting from one wood to another – they don't like crossing open fields.

The bad news for farmers is that fields that are unprotected by hedges can be eroded by the wind, which can blow away valuable topsoil.

OVER TO YOU

If you live near a hedge, you need to take responsibility for it.

• If you see litter in hedges and can safely remove it, do so. Did you know that if small animals, such as hedgehogs, push their noses in to the opening of empty drinks cans, they get stuck, and are unable to pull their noses out? Ouch.

• Don't let anyone go overboard with the hedge-trimmer if
you have a hedge or trees on which berries grow.
Birds' lives may depend on eating those berries.

• Don't let anyone tidy up the fallen leaves and long grass
at the bottom of the hedge. This provides shelter for animals.

• Ban the gardeners in your family from using harmful
herbicides – they may find their way into your hedge and
poison the wildlife.

• Start a 'Fences Are Boring' campaign. Encourage people
to plant hedges in their gardens. (If you plant a hedge in
your garden, be careful not to go over your neighbour's
boundary lines – get your parents to check this out.)

No.25: Protect Local Birds

As cities grow, and fields and park areas are built on and grass disappears under patios, paving and decking, many birds have found themselves homeless and hungry.

OVER TO YOU

Here are some of the ways you can help the birds who live near you.

• Provide your bird pals something they can use as a bath – birds need to keep their feathers clean to keep warm.
Put out an old baking tray or a large pottery bowl and fill it with clean water.

• Build a bird a home using a large, empty, plastic milk container or a soup carton with holes the size of an eggcup cut through them. Put some shredded paper or straw inside the container to be used as bedding.

• If you have a garden, tell your family to think twice about digging up the lawn and replacing it with gravel, a patio, or decking. All the insects and worms that lived in that grass will be killed and garden birds will go hungry.

• Don't use pesticides on plants and insects.
Birds may eat them.

No.26: Birds Love Leftovers

Did you know that, on average, each person in Europe throws away the equivalent of 2,800 banana skins in food waste every year? As well as seeds and nuts, birds are happy to be offered most kitchen leftovers. So never let anyone in your household throw away any leftover food without checking this list first.

• cakes • biscuits • bread • crumbled cheese • pasta
• cooked rice • pastry • bacon rind • old fruit • potatoes
• unsalted nuts • fat from meat • bones
(Do NOT give birds salted nuts or desiccated coconut.)

Put up a feeding table on a balcony or in a garden area. Make sure it is somewhere out of the reach of hungry cats.

Local birds will soon identify your table as a reliable source of food, so don't forget to keep feeding them through the winter.

No.27: Make A Composter

A lot of kitchen and garden waste is organic matter, which in other words is stuff that was once alive. If you were to make a heap of it outdoors, in just a few days it would be visited by bacteria, algae and fungi, which will cause it to rot. Worms, beetles and maggots make a tasty meal of all the rotting matter, leaving lots of tiny little pieces that we call compost. Pretty GROSS, but compost is a very good fertiliser for gardens.

OVER TO YOU

• Build or buy a compost container and put it in the garden. Composts need to be warm and damp, so a sunny, sheltered spot is ideal.

• A composter loves all grass and plant cuttings from your garden. It loves the peelings you have from fruit and vegetables, but don't add meat, cheese or fish, or you may encourage rats into your garden.

• Keep a container into which the things listed on page 49 can be emptied ready for composting. Check no one is putting these things in the rubbish bin instead.

• When the composter collection box is full take it out into the garden and empty it into the composter. Two-thirds of the household rubbish we put in our dustbins could be composted. Copy out the list below and stick it on your fridge to remind people what goes in the compost box.

FEED ME
• grass cuttings • hair cuttings • hay • straw • hedge trimmings • non-coloured paper • tea bags • vegetable peelings • leftover vegetables • leftover fruit • coffee grounds • cut up newspaper • cardboard

• Finally, feel free to wee on your compost heap, but only occasionally. Some people think this is a really good idea, although others think it makes the compost rather acidic.

No.28: When To Watch Worms

Why not buy your household a wormery or add worms to your compost heap? Worms love to eat tea bags, coffee-grounds and soggy cardboard. They even like newspaper when it has been torn into tasty strips. Watch while your worms turn your household waste into wonderful compost that will help your garden grow.

Chapter Three

Shopping for the Planet

Did you know that many people in Europe throw away six times their body weight in rubbish every year? All that rubbish has to be put somewhere. Most of it is buried underground in landfill sites. This means our planet is in danger of becoming one big rubbish tip.

The easiest way to deal with the huge problem of rubbish is sensible shopping – buy less stuff, which means less waste packaging and less waste to throw away.

No.29: Shopping Lists

It's essential to monitor your household's weekly shopping lists and make sure that it only includes things that will last, rather than things that will soon be thrown away.
Here are some classic examples:

BUY-TO-THROW LIST

- disposable nappies

- plastic biros

- plastic razors

- paper towels

- paper tissues

- plastic food bags

- paper tablecloths and napkins, plastic plates and straws

BUY-TO-KEEP LIST

- cloth nappies

- one good pen

- a non-disposable razor

- washable dishcloths

- linen hankies

- plastic food containers

- washable or wipe-down tablecloths, china plates, linen napkins

No.30: Just Say No

Don't let anyone in your family be seduced into buying things because of cool adverts or pretty packaging. Tell them that supermarkets will try anything to get you to buy more than you need. For example, '2 for 1' offers aren't a bargain if you only need one or you don't need any at all!

The best way to stop the members of your family falling into these traps is to make sure that anyone going shopping takes a shopping list. The list will only include items your household actually needs.

The highest point in Ohio, USA, is said to be 'Mount Rumpke' – a mountain made of trash.

No:31: Avoid Food Miles

When you jump in the car to head to the shops, it's not just the petrol your car uses that is being consumed. Goods that travel long distances to shops need boats and planes to transport them. The emissions of these, in turn, pollute our oceans and skies. This is why we talk about 'food miles'. Ideally we do not want too many 'miles' on our plate.

Food Miles

Food miles are a measure of how far our food has to travel to get it from the place where it was grown to our plate. The further it comes, the more energy it takes to transport it.

FOOD MILES

OVER TO YOU

• Always check out the country of origin on the labels of food products and of clothes before you buy them. Do you *need* to buy a pair of pyjamas that were made in China? Check a map . . . that's too many miles.

• Try to buy food grown locally. If a farm near to you grows apples, why would you buy apples that need to be imported from New Zealand? Check a map . . . all the way from New Zealand . . . that's too many food miles.

• Eat foods that are in season in your country. Don't buy strawberries in the winter if they have been flown across the Atlantic. Check a map . . . all the way from the USA . . . that's too many food miles.

• Join a local organic fruit-and-vegetable box scheme. Check a map . . . one truck bringing local produce to the doors of several customers uses less petrol than each of those people driving to the supermarket.

• Grow your own food. It's fun and it's green. Check a map . . . food miles from your vegetable patch to your plate . . . only a few paces.

• Don't buy food that you do not need. Check a map . . . food miles of something you don't buy . . . zero.

However, green issues are never simple. Some people feel that farmers in countries such as Africa will suffer if Europeans, attempting to avoid food miles, don't buy their produce.

No.32: Say No To Bottled Water

Don't be dumb enough to think bottled water is better for you than drinking tap water. Here's why:

THE FACTS

- Bottled water is not tested for impurities to the same high standards as tap water.

- Plastic water bottles can take hundreds of years to decay and just create more litter in dumps and landfill sites.

- Dentists think that tap water is better for you as it often contains fluoride, which helps to strengthen your teeth.

No.33: Always Read The Label

Some innocent-looking household products contain harmful chemicals, so make sure you always read the label of the products you buy. Look out for products that promise to be kinder to the environment.

Another thing to look out for is proof that an item's packaging has been made from recycled paper or plastic.

No.34: Shopping For Greens

Next time someone heads to the supermarket, get them to read and agree to the shopping contract shown below.

OUR FAMILY SHOPPING CONTRACT

• **Our household will do only one BIG shop a week.**
This will encourage us not to buy unwanted food, and we will use less petrol getting to and from the supermarket.

• **Whenever possible we will choose organic foods farmed without the use of chemicals.**
This is better for the Earth and is probably better for us, too.

• **Whenever possible we'll buy food from local producers.**
It uses up less fuel to transport this food to the supermarket.

• **We will buy fruit and vegetables in season.**
('In season' means at the time of year they naturally grow.)
We check the labels to see what country they have come from and resist stuff that has been flown halfway around the world.

No.35: Eat Fruit, Don't Drink Juices

Ready-made fruit juices contain lots of sugar, but, worse still, the production of fruit juices requires both huge amounts of packaging and huge amounts of water.

By eating real fruit you will save your teeth, save water, save energy, save food miles, and prevent even more rubbish ending up in landfill sites.

OVER TO YOU

• Buy organic fruit from local farms or farmers' markets. This cuts down both on the pesticides polluting the planet and the petrol used in transport.

• If you only like fruit in the form of juice, dig out the juicer you never use and make your own.

• Don't forget to compost all your peelings and any fruit that gets overripe and too old to eat (see page 48) .

No.36: Buy In Bulk

This book has taught you to buy only the things you need, and never to buy more than you need. However, when you buy essential items it is a good idea to buy them in the largest containers you can find. This is called buying in bulk. Buying in bulk means fewer car trips to the shops, which means less petrol and pollution. It means less packaging, too. Plus the good news is bulk buying is often cheaper.

It's *soooo* much better buying small packets of food, because there's less waste.

Durrrr!

Actually, bulk buying reduces packaging, not the other way around. For example, one large cereal box is made from less cardboard than two small ones. Squash the boxes flat and measure them if you like.

However, steer clear of big bags of individually-wrapped sweets or crisp packets. These have extra packaging. The same goes for bottles of water or other multi-buy goods that are bound together with plastic wrapping.

No.37: Fast Food Is Forbidden

We all know by now that fast food isn't good for us, but did you know it isn't very good for the planet, either?

Fast-food restaurants often individually wrap their food. Just think of all the packaging you get when you buy a burger – the burger is in a box, the fries in a bag, the drink is in a polystyrene cup, the salt, the pepper and the sauces come in sachets and there's often paper napkins, plastic cutlery and a straw all thrown into another big bag so you can carry it all.

And what do people do the minute they leave the shop? They throw away all the packaging – hopefully in the bin, but sometimes on the pavement.

Plastic packaging material does not decompose for hundreds of years (see page 77) and is cluttering up our landfill sites. Meanwhile, rubbish left on our streets attracts rats that may spread disease.

OVER TO YOU

• Try to eat in cafes and restaurants where food is served on a china plate with metal cutlery. These can be used again and again. If you can't resist fast food, put the packaging into your recycling bin, and at least say no to the free plastic toy – you will just end up throwing it away.

No.38: Be A Trendsetter Not A Fashion Victim

Before you check out a new pair of jeans, check this out:

FACTS ABOUT OUR CLOTHES

• The clothing, shoe and textile industry uses huge amounts of oil and electricity. It uses more water than any other industry (apart from agriculture).

• Most of our clothes are made from cotton. Cotton production is responsible for using more than ¼ of the world's pesticides that pollute our soil and our rivers.

• 30% of the chemicals used in clothes manufacturing can harm our health.

OVER TO YOU

• Copy out the clothing contract shown on the next page and stick it on your wardrobe door.

CLOTHING CONTRACT

• I won't be a fashion victim
at the expense of my planet!

• I will wear a hemp sack from now on ...
actually this may be going too far, but I promise
to buy fewer clothes – only the ones I really need.

• I will buy some clothes made from organic materials.
Check out online which designers are going organic.

• I will give all the clothes that don't fit me to charity.

• Holes can be mended or patched up.
I will keep patches in fashion!

• I will wear the jumper Granny knitted for me.
If it is too bad I will put it on my compost heap.

No. 39: Dry-Cleaning Ban

When you send clothes to the dry-cleaners chemicals are used to get out the stains. Unfortunately these chemicals (known as volatile organic compounds or VOCs) make stains on our planet which are harder to remove. In fact, they turn our skies brown. Check out these dirty facts:

DIRTY FACTS ABOUT DRY-CLEANING

• VOCs mix with nitrogen oxides in the atmosphere, where they react to form ozone at ground level. This appears as a brownish haze.

• The chemical tetrachloroethylene that is used in dry-cleaning can cause cancer in animals.

• When you pick up your clothes from the dry-cleaners they may still retain low levels of tetrachloroethylene that you might breathe in when you wear them.

• Dry-cleaners put clean clothes on metal hangers and put them in plastic bags – really wasteful!

So, if anyone in your family is about to buy an item of clothing that is dry-clean only, make sure they know the effect it will have on the planet.

No.40: Are They A Green Team?

Some clothes designers and retailers are trying to help our planet by using organic materials and dyes that are kinder to the environment. Why not write a letter like this one to your favourite shop and see just how green they are?

To the Manager of [my favourite shop]

Dear Sir/Madam

I have bought loads of wicked clothes from you this year, as I like the things you sell. However, I have heard that the fashion industry also does some wicked things to this planet (I mean 'bad things' this time, by the way).

Could you tell me if you:
a) stock clothes made from organic cotton?
b) use any recycled materials?
c) use any chemicals that are bad for my skin or the environment?

Thanks. I'll wait to hear from you before buying anything else from your shop.

Yours faithfully

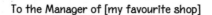

No.41: Don't Harm Hardwood Trees

The next time your family wants to buy a new piece of furniture, make it your job to find out what it is made from. If that tempting table is made from a tree grown on a plantation, or from reclaimed wood, this means it is OK to buy it.

However, if it is made from a hardwood, such as teak or mahogany, that originated in an endangered forest, just say NO. You can help keep those ancient trees standing.

65

OVER TO YOU

• Look to see if items made from wood (not only furniture but paper products too) come with an 'FSC' label. The Forest Stewardship Council guarantees that the wood used in these products comes from sustainable forests. Large furniture companies like Home Depot and IKEA now source wood from these forests. This book is printed on FSC paper.

• Don't buy furniture that has been made to look antique, instead buy real antiques – buying second-hand items prevents trees from being cut down to make new furniture.

• Do not dump useful furniture – someone else could take it off your hands. Take it to a charity shop or even an auction.

HARD FACTS

Hardwoods like mahogany and teak are very valuable, and may have taken 500 or more years to grow. As a result the wood can be sold for a great profit. Tree poaching by stealth loggers is a common practice, even in protected forests.

In the search for these valuable trees, forest areas the size of football pitches are cleared or damaged every day. The forests in which they have been felled may never recover.

No.42: Don't Be A Gadget Geek

New gadgets and toys are fun to play with . . . well, they are at first. But are they really useful?

Make a spreadsheet that lists each unused gadget in your household. Sit your family down and get them to confess when they last used each item.

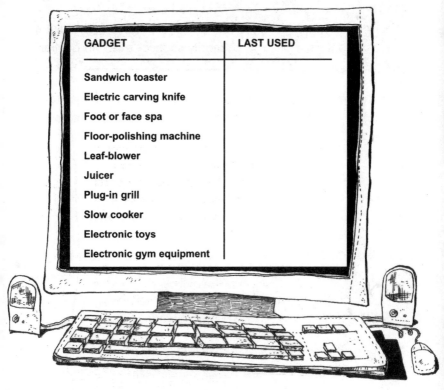

GADGET	LAST USED
Sandwich toaster	
Electric carving knife	
Foot or face spa	
Floor-polishing machine	
Leaf-blower	
Juicer	
Plug-in grill	
Slow cooker	
Electronic toys	
Electronic gym equipment	

Use your spreadsheet to work out which gadgets are no longer used by your family. Don't throw them away, but instead take them to a car-boot sale, a charity shop or perhaps sell them on eBay. You don't want someone else buying a new useless gadget if they can take yours.

Finally, make your family promise to think hard before buying gadgets that may end up lying around the house unused.

No.43: Use Energy-Efficient Appliances

If your parents are about to set off and buy a new household appliance, insist on going with them – you have a serious job to do.

Make sure they pick energy-efficient appliances. For example, using an energy-efficient fridge could save half a tonne of CO_2 a year compared to an older model.

You should be able to find out specific information on how energy-efficient an appliance is in the shop before you buy. Look out for an energy-efficiency logo or a label on the appliance detailing its energy consumption.

Failing this, ask the store assistant if they can provide this information, and don't take no for an answer.

No.44: Use Appliances Efficiently

Always ensure that any appliance in your house is not only energy-efficient but that it is being used efficiently by your family. For example, your fridge could be responsible for about 20% of your household's electricity use.

Take a look at your fridge and fill in this questionnaire:

FRIDGE QUESTIONNAIRE

	YES	NO
Is our fridge set to the correct temperature as stated in the manual?	☐	☐
Is our fridge kept well stocked? (Did you know a half-full fridge or freezer uses more energy than a full one?)	☐	☐
Is the fridge located in a good place? (It will use more energy if it is placed next to a radiator or the oven.)	☐	☐
Is the fridge defrosted regularly? (If not, the freezer compartment door may not shut properly, and this means the fridge will not work efficiently.)	☐	☐

If your family buys a new fridge or freezer, always make sure the old one is disposed of responsibly.

If there is nothing wrong with it, see if someone else wants it.

Chlorofluorocarbons, or CFCs, are chemicals used in refrigeration and air-conditioning units and products such as aerosol sprays. When they get into the air, CFCs destroy ozone (see below). Removing CFCs from fridges requires specialist equipment. If your fridge is really past its best take it to your local rubbish and recycling centre or have it collected by your local council so that it can be disposed of properly.

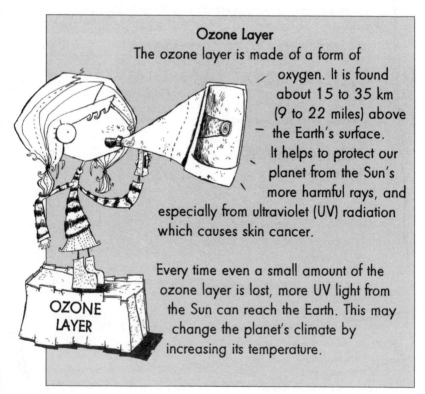

Ozone Layer
The ozone layer is made of a form of oxygen. It is found about 15 to 35 km (9 to 22 miles) above the Earth's surface. It helps to protect our planet from the Sun's more harmful rays, and especially from ultraviolet (UV) radiation which causes skin cancer.

Every time even a small amount of the ozone layer is lost, more UV light from the Sun can reach the Earth. This may change the planet's climate by increasing its temperature.

OZONE LAYER

No.45: Have A Green Christmas

Dear Santa,

As the perfect end to a perfect green year, I would like to request the following green gifts for Christmas:

• A bird table (made out of reclaimed wood)

• A wormery and/or mini-composter

• Proper wool socks to keep me warm around the house

• Organic cotton pyjamas so fewer chemicals get into the environment.

Love from me

P.S. Will you sponsor an endangered animal for me?

No. 46: Give Green Gifts

Here's a project for truly committed eco-warriors . . . at Christmas and birthdays resist the temptation to ask for loads of presents. Ask yourself how much you really appreciated all the things people bought you last year. Chances are you will have forgotten, broken, or got bored with at least some of the gifts.

This year don't get throwaway presents. Ask for a trip to the zoo, a football match or the movies.

Oh, and don't tarnish your green halo by showering your loved ones with offerings either. Give good deeds. Wash your dad's car. Tidy Granny's garden. Clear out the garage.

No.47: Make Your Own Products

Many products we use every day contain chemicals that are harmful to the environment. Some are not great for *us* either – the chemicals in them can be absorbed into our bodies through our skin. The chemicals also end up in our water supply and get in to our food chain, so we end up drinking and eating them later on.

Why not make your own products using natural ingredients? Take hair conditioners for example – you can buy eco-friendly brands or make your own using the recipes shown below. Only wash and condition your hair when it really needs it.

When you do wash your hair try using smaller quantities of shampoo and conditioner. It is better for your hair and better for the environment.

Conditioner

Mash up an avocado. Mix it up with mayonnaise.

Spread the mixture all over your freshly washed hair.

Rinse thoroughly.

Conditioner

Use a blender to blend one teaspoon of honey, one egg yolk, two tablespoons of olive oil.

Work the mixture into clean hair and leave for thirty minutes before shampooing.

chapter four

Reduce, Reuse, Repair, Recycle

Our planet has a 'finite' amount of resources. This means that they are limited and that we can't replace the materials we have taken from the planet with new ones.
All the metal, gems, coal and oil we take out of the ground every day took millions of years to form. When they are used up, there won't be any more for us to take.

This is why it's so important that we don't buy anything we don't need, we don't waste, that we repair and reuse as much as possible, and failing all else, we recycle absolutely everything we can.

No.48: Make A Dumper's Diary

It's time to take a closer look at the rubbish your household is throwing out . . . a smelly job but someone has to do it. Check your household bins and start a dumper's diary, noting down the following things:

DUMPER'S DIARY

This week we threw out .... bags of rubbish.

The following things could have been recycled:

_____

The following things could have been reused:

_____

The following things could have been put
on the compost heap:

_____

The following things should not have
been bought in the first place:

_____

No.49: Make A Decay Diary

To make sure people understand just how long rubbish in landfill sites takes to biodegrade, perform the following experiment. Find a piece of land on which you have permission to dig. Make a hole and bury some or all of the following items:

- an apple • a banana • eggshells • a tea bag
- an old shoe • a woolly hat or glove • a newspaper advertisement • a toilet-roll tube • a tin can
- a crisp packet • a plastic bottle • a plastic carrier bag

Visit your experiment site regularly. Uncover the items and notice what changes have occurred between visits. Write down how long each item takes to decompose.

Check out the following depressing decay data:

- a sheet of paper will take 2 to 5 months to decay.
- orange peel will take 6 months to decay.
- a milk carton will take 5 years to decay.
- a cigarette butt will take 10 years to decay.
- a tin can will take 100 years to decay.
- an aluminium can will take 200 to 500 years to decay.
- a plastic six-pack cover will take 450 years to decay.
- a plastic bag will take 500 to 1,000 years to decay.
- a polystyrene cup will NEVER decay!

No.50: Recycle Glass Bottles And Jars

Huge furnaces all over the world can each produce more than a million glass bottles and jars every day. Think how many of those containers are littering our planet. It is essential to recycle all the glass bottles and jars that come into your house.

FACTS WITH A LOT OF BOTTLE

• Recycling glass saves natural resources like sand, soda ash and limestone.

• Recycling glass creates less pollution than producing new jars and bottles does. The energy saved by recycling one glass bottle could power a 100-watt light bulb for almost an hour, power a computer for 25 minutes, and power a colour TV for 20 minutes.

• The amazing thing about glass is that it can be recycled forever.

Before putting jars and bottles in the glass bank, rinse them, remove any lids and tops, and sort them into clear, green and brown glass.

No.51: Can The Cans

In 2001, three billion aluminium cans ended up in landfill sites in the UK. These cans will take thousands of years to decompose. It's up to you to take action – recycle them.

Instead of tower blocks on the surface of the planet, we are in danger of ending up with towers of rubbish underground!

79

OVER TO YOU

• Do you really need all those fizzy drinks? The answer is NO. Switch to a reusable, refillable bottle of water instead.

• Buy fresh fruit and vegetables, not tinned. Don't let your family stock cupboards with cans of fruit and soup that never see the light of day.

No.52: No One Wants A Six-Pack

When you buy canned drinks are they held together by plastic holders? Do they have ring-pulls to open them? If so, cut up the six-pack holders before disposing of them. Separate the ring-pulls from cans completely and crush the cans flat before they go in the bin. Animals and birds die from being trapped in or strangled by six-pack holders and cans.

80

No.53: Devise A Recycling System

Take a trip to your local rubbish and recycling centre. Make a note of what is thrown away and what can be recycled. In most countries recyclable materials include glass, tins, plastic, paper, and cardboard. In some areas people are even encouraged to recycle clothing and shoes.

OVER TO YOU

Make it your job to set up a recycling system tailor-made for your household:

• Find out which materials are recycled in your area. Check whether they are collected from your house or whether you have to take them to a collection point.

• Write a list of all the items your household must recycle from now on. Make sure everyone reads it and then stick it up near your household bins.

• Some local authorities provide special bins and bags for different categories of recyclable materials. If your local authority doesn't do this, you can make a selection of labelled boxes for each category of material. Again, make sure everyone knows what goes where.

• Monitor your family's recycling efforts carefully.

No.54: Swap Shop

When was the last time you cleared out the toys, books, computer games, CDs or DVDs you just didn't want any more? Before buying any new ones, make sure you recycle the old ones. Unless they are broken beyond repair, DO NOT put them in the bin. Send them to a jumble sale, give them to a charity shop, or why not sell them on eBay or at a car-boot fair and make some money?

Alternatively, get DVDs and books from the library, or swap your unwanted stuff with things your mates no longer want. Someone else's unwanted goods may be your lucky find!

No.55: Reuse And Recycle Paper

Do you know what we throw away the most of? The answer is paper and card. The average person uses and disposes of the equivalent of seven trees a year.

This is crazy, because reusing and recycling paper is something that we can all do very easily – and it works. Moreover, making recycled paper instead of cutting down trees to make new paper uses 64% less energy and 58% less water.

OVER TO YOU

Here's how to reduce the amount of paper your family uses:

- Always use both sides of a piece of paper and use scraps for shopping lists.

- Get your family to use a chalkboard to leave messages for each other instead of sticky notes.

- Always print on both sides of a sheet of paper. Put an empty box beside your computer's printer to collect up old printouts for re-use.

- Buy as many of your books as you can from car-boot fairs or in second-hand shops.

• Share books and magazines with your friends.

• Always try to buy things made from recycled paper, such as toilet rolls, kitchen rolls, writing paper, wrapping paper and notepads.

• Tear up wastepaper items such as dirty kitchen towels and add them to your compost bin. (Newspaper can go in too, but beware of adding glossy magazines whose inks may contain nasty toxins.)

• Every single newspaper, sheet of paper or card that can't be reused or composted must go into the recycling box. Did you know that if we recycled all our newspapers we would save about 250 million trees a year?

No.56: Junk Your Junk Mail

Junk mail is mail sent by companies who want your business but whom you didn't ask to be contacted by. It has become a huge headache for the people who have to dispose of it. Most junk mail is thrown away without even being read.

OVER TO YOU

• Sign up to a 'Mailing Preference Service' to opt out of receiving junk mail. Alternatively, contact your postal service and request you only receive mail actually addressed to a member of your family.

• When filling in forms or subscriptions, look out for a box which offers you future promotions or mail from other sources. If you don't want it, make sure you let them know.

• Make sure everyone in your house opts to receive sales and marketing information by e-mail rather than by post.

• Put up a big note like the one below on your front door for all those pesky people who pop leaflets and adverts through your letterbox.

Absolutely NO junk mail, thank you. We mean it!

No.57: Cut Out The Cards

It's wonderful to get a card from far-away family and friends, but do we really need all those birthday and Christmas cards? Every year hundreds of thousands of trees are chopped down just to make Christmas cards, and billions of those cards get put in the bin straight after Christmas.

OVER TO YOU

• Use your computer to design greetings cards. Don't print them out, e-mail them. This saves paper, saves the fuel the post office uses to deliver them and saves you money on stamps. If you aren't feeling creative or inspired, lots of websites offer ready-made e-cards with music and pictures.

• If you really want to give a card to someone in your family or class at school, suggest presenting one card and getting everyone to sign it. This avoids lots of individual cards and envelopes.

No.58: Make Your Own Christmas Decoration

Don't let your family get carried away next Christmas with all the glittery, plastic cards and decorations you see in the shops. They can't be recycled. So make your own. How about using things that you, or the birds in your garden, can eat later?

- Thread together popcorn and peanuts (in their shells).

- Make tree decorations from dough or gingerbread, tangerines decorated with cloves, or cut up old cardboard packaging. All these can be composted when Christmas is over.

- Decorate your home with holly or evergreen branches, not tinsel. Don't cut down too much as you may damage trees or upset the habitat of local wildlife. Avoid cutting down holly with berries. This looks nice, but we can't eat the berries, while birds can. Be careful with mistletoe as some species are now endangered. Compost all the greenery afterwards.

No.59: Reuse Envelopes

Open envelopes carefully so they don't get too torn. Then you can cover the old address and stamps with sticky labels. Next time you need to post a letter, use one of your recycled envelopes. Keep some sticky tape handy for resealing them.

Oh, and don't throw away the envelopes you damaged in your excitement to open them. Gather a stack of them, punch a hole through the corner and tie them together with a ribbon to make a notepad.

No.60: Recycle Your Shoes

Put an old trainer on the compost heap, and see just how long it takes to decompose . . .

. . . on second thoughts, don't. You might find a family of bugs living in it, but you would have to stare at it for a long, long time to see it decompose. Now think of the millions of trainers and other shoes that get dumped in landfill sites every day. Each year in the UK alone, shoppers purchase over 260 million pairs of new shoes.

OVER TO YOU

• Many shoes that are thrown away have little wrong with them. Make sure you take good-as-new or hardly-worn trainers to friends, the charity shops or a shoe bank. Why not get everyone at school to collect up unwanted shoes and trainers? Before you send your shoes anywhere, tie them together so they stay in pairs.

What happens to the shoes put in the shoe bank?

Some are sent abroad. Others are used in schemes like the one set up in 1993 by the sports company Nike called Reuse-A-Shoe. Old sports shoes are ground up to create a material which is used to make running tracks, court surfaces, and children's playgrounds.

No.61: When Is It Cool To Be An Old Bag?

Carrier bags, made from a plastic called polyethylene, are the single biggest polluters of our planet. About 100 billion plastic bags are thrown away in the USA every year, and in the UK the average person uses 134 bags every year.

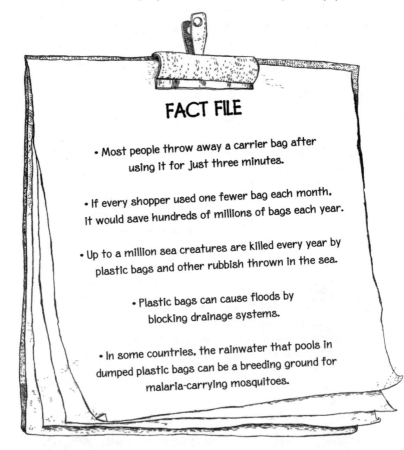

FACT FILE

• Most people throw away a carrier bag after using it for just three minutes.

• If every shopper used one fewer bag each month, it would save hundreds of millions of bags each year.

• Up to a million sea creatures are killed every year by plastic bags and other rubbish thrown in the sea.

• Plastic bags can cause floods by blocking drainage systems.

• In some countries, the rainwater that pools in dumped plastic bags can be a breeding ground for malaria-carrying mosquitoes.

OVER TO YOU

• Buy some strong bags that can be taken to the supermarket every week.

• Buy your household some 'Bags For Life' (strong, reusable plastic bags) and make sure nobody hits the shops without them.

• Buy loose fruit and vegetables, not stuff that has been put in polystyrene trays wrapped in plastic. Then make sure you don't undo all your good work by putting them in a plastic bag – they can go straight in your shopping basket.

• If you do take a plastic bag home, make sure you reuse it next time you go shopping.

It's soooo much better to use paper bags instead of plastic bags.

Durrrr!

No. In fact it takes more than four times as much energy to manufacture a paper bag as it does to manufacture a plastic bag.

No.62: A Bag Is For Life

Write a letter like the one below to your local supermarket and tell them exactly what you require of them. Get your friends to write in too.

Dear Sir/Madam

It is essential that we reduce the number of plastic bags used in this world.

There are two things I'd like you, my local supermarket, to do:

1. Provide a 'Bag for Life' scheme for customers.

2. Charge customers for every ordinary plastic bag they use.

In countries where supermarkets charge for plastic bags there has been a 90% reduction in their use.

Yours faithfully

No.63: A Wheelie Good Idea

SNUB unnecessary carrier bags. (That's 'Say No to Unnecessary Bags'.)

Why not buy your household a wheelie bag that can be taken on every shopping trip? Go on – start a trend.

No.64: Refill Not Refuse

Did you know that a third of all the rubbish in rubbish dumps is old packaging?

Companies are developing plastics that will decompose, made from sugar and other carbohydrates. These rot away within months of being buried. Unfortunately, these cost a lot more money to produce. So we need to avoid packaging as much as possible.

OVER TO YOU

• Look out for products that come in containers that can be refilled. This means that you can use the same container again and again.

• Why not buy your family some travel cups that they can get filled in a coffee shop instead of their being given polystyrene cups?

• Don't buy plastic disposable items, such as cameras, plastic razors, picnic plates and cutlery. They all end up in landfill sites. Make sure you buy things that will last.

• If you can't avoid packaging, choose cardboard rather than plastic.

No.65: Recycle Your Mobile

In Europe 100 million mobile phones are discarded every year. Only 5% of these phones are recycled. The rest end up in landfill sites where the metals they contain (including gold and silver) are wasted. They also contain toxic substances, such as cadmium, mercury, lead and arsenic, which can leak into the soil. Ingesting just small quantities of lead can damage our kidneys, liver, brain, heart, blood and nerves, cause memory loss, and affect behaviour and reproduction.

OVER TO YOU

- If your phone is still working – don't upgrade it.

- When you do want to upgrade, contact a charity, such as Oxfam, who will reuse or recycle your phone. Alternatively, find a site on the Web that will recycle your phone and send you money for it.

- Why not start a collection scheme at school for old phones? You'll be amazed how many phones are hidden at the bottom of drawers in every household.

Did you know that leakage from just one mobile phone battery can pollute 158,000 gallons of water?

No.66: Better Batteries

Most standard batteries contain hazardous substances that may leak into the soil if they end up in landfill sites. Invest in rechargeable batteries with a charger. They can be used again and again before they need to be disposed of.

No.67: Recycle Your Ink Cartridges And Computers

Don't let anyone you know throw away a computer just because they think it is out of date. Someone else might be glad to have it.

If you do get rid of a computer, take it to your local rubbish and recycling centre so it is disposed of properly. Computers contain dangerous chemicals that may leak into the soil.

Don't forget to recycle your ink cartridges too. Leaking ink can also pollute the environment, and the plastic they're made of will take many years to decompose.

Look on the Web for charitable organisations that collect and recycle printer cartridges, thereby keeping them out of landfill sites. The money they raise is used to help the world's poorest and most vulnerable people.

No.68: Reuse Your Rubbish Creatively

Here are some ideas of how to be a creative recycler.

Paint empty cereal boxes and stick them together to make a paper-filing system.

Decorate jam jars with enamel paints and put tea lights inside them to illuminate the garden when you have a night-time BBQ.

Cut up the cardboard tube found inside loo roll. Paint them to make napkin rings.

Decorate old ice-cream tubs with paint and glitter. Use them to store anything from pasta to pens.

Hang old CDS on a string to add sparkle to your bedroom.

Decorate some old CD cases and make them into photo frames.

Chapter Five
Stop Polluting The Planet

Poisonous emissions are destroying the planet. These emissions include the toxic chemicals that factories pump into the sky and the waste that is dumped into rivers. They include the gases given off by planes and cars that transport people around the world.

The amount of emissions polluting our planet increases every day.

You need to look at the way your family treats and travels the planet, to ensure that you don't leave our Earth a dirtier place than you found it.

No.69: Save Our Seaside

Our seas are becoming dangerously polluted with harmful chemicals and sewage. Marine plants and animals and even people who are just paddling at the seaside are suffering.

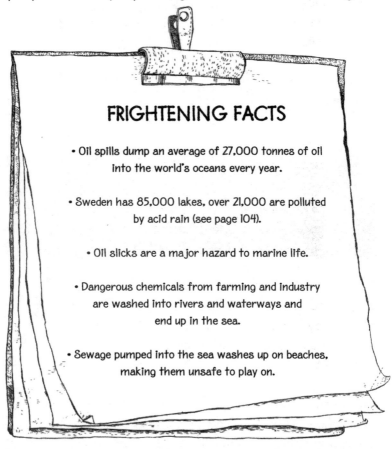

FRIGHTENING FACTS

• Oil spills dump an average of 27,000 tonnes of oil into the world's oceans every year.

• Sweden has 85,000 lakes, over 21,000 are polluted by acid rain (see page 104).

• Oil slicks are a major hazard to marine life.

• Dangerous chemicals from farming and industry are washed into rivers and waterways and end up in the sea.

• Sewage pumped into the sea washes up on beaches, making them unsafe to play on.

OVER TO YOU

Play your own part in keeping the seaside safe:

• Make sure that you don't leave any rubbish behind you on the beach. Always take it home with you. Carrier bags and balloons, for example, are a danger to sea creatures. If they blow into the water they can be mistaken for food by marine life. Once eaten these materials may fool the creatures into thinking their stomachs are full and they will starve.

• If you live near the sea, join a conservation group that gets together to clean up beaches. Your local library will have more information.

No.70: Save Our Streams

If you don't live by the sea, help to protect local rivers, ponds and lakes instead. Our waterways can become blocked by branches and rubbish that is thrown into them. If water can't flow freely it becomes stagnant, and creatures and plants will die.

You'll find organisations dedicated to looking after streams, lakes and rivers in your area. Getting involved is not only a great way to help the environment, but you'll also meet other cool people who are actively saving the planet.

No.71: Save Our School

Set up a club at school to protect a local area of natural beauty. If there isn't an obvious area of natural beauty nearby, such as a river, a forest or a beach, why not choose to protect your school playing field?

Organise teams of friends to clear up the litter people have dropped. Talk to your school's caretaker about using environmentally friendly ways of killing pests and weeds. Perhaps you could explain how much water is wasted by watering the grass during a hot summer.

No.72: Methane Alert . . . Be Aware

Getting to the bottom of the matter, animals such as sheep and cows produce methane from burping and farting. The bad news is that methane is a greenhouse gas (see page 20).

As the Earth's population grows, more agricultural animals are needed to produce clothing and food – which means more burping and farting – which means more methane – which means more harmful greenhouse gases.

OVER TO YOU

• Eat less meat to reduce the need to breed so many farting animals.

• Buy fewer new clothes and whenever possible choose clothes made from recycled material. If everyone in the UK bought just one jumper made from recycled wool, it would save 371 million gallons of water, 480 tonnes of chemical dyes and 4,751 million days of an average family's electricity needs. Australia alone has 114 million wool- and methane-producing sheep.

• Punish anyone found farting – only joking!

Scientists estimate that 14% of methane comes from farting farm animals. This means cows can cause more pollution than cars.

Oops. Pardon me!

No.73: Reduce Acid Rain

When power stations, factories and cars burn fuel, greenhouse gases escape into the air. Some of these gases react with droplets of water in clouds to form sulphuric and nitric acids, which is how we get acid rain.

ACID RAIN FACT FILE:

• Acid rain is polluting lakes and rivers and killing wildlife. In Scandinavia, lakes which seem crystal clear are known as 'dead lakes'. Thanks to acid rain they now contain no living creatures or plants.

• Acid rain destroys trees and forests. It can increase the acidity of soil so that trees can't grow. It can dissolve and wash away vital nutrients and minerals in the soil. It can damage the waxy protective coating of leaves, which may prevent them from being able to photosynthesize properly.

• Acid rain is eroding ancient statues and damaging buildings – it will even damage your car if it is left outside.

The best way for you to help with acid rain is to take all the advice in this book about saving fuel and conserving energy.

Oh, and if you do leave the car at home, better put it in the garage in case it rains acid!

No.74: Park The Car

Did you know that most of the journeys people make in their car are fewer than FIVE miles? This means they could easily walk or cycle. Perhaps they don't know that, on average, every gallon of petrol used by a car puts about 9 kg (20 lb) of CO_2 into the atmosphere.

It's essential to avoid unnecessary trips. Persuade your family to leave the car at home when possible. Why not challenge them to manage without the car for a whole weekend?

No.75: Make Pool Pals

Talk to all the friends who live near you and go to the same school. Can you organise a car pool for the school run? A car pool means each household takes a turn in driving a car FULL of kids to school. Why not work out a rota for your 'pool pals'?

Car pooling is a great way to save energy and reduce emissions of greenhouse gases. Persuade your parents to car pool with their colleagues at work.

No.76: Get To Know Your Family

About 12% of the greenhouse gases that cause global warming are produced by transport. So it's time to monitor your family's travelling habits and transport decisions.

Start with your family car. Watch your parents driving habits. Do they drive smoothly? Do they turn off the engine when they stop for more than 30 seconds at traffic lights? Is the car boot empty of everything but essentials? All these sensible driving practices can significantly reduce the amount of fuel a car consumes.

You must also tell your parents to get their car serviced regularly. A smooth running engine emits fewer nasty substances. If all car owners serviced their vehicles regularly, millions of kilograms of CO_2 would be eliminated from the atmosphere. Make sure they get the garage to check that the tyres are properly inflated, because under-inflated tyres use up more energy. Make sure they check that the air-conditioning system is not leaking dangerous chemicals into the air.

Get your parents to fill in the questionnaire overleaf to see how green they are when it comes to cars. The more times they answer YES, the more they need to change their driving habits.

	YES	NO
1. Does your family own a car that only does a kilometre per litre/gallon of petrol?	☐	☐
2. Does it seem like the car is always in use?	☐	☐
3. Is your car more than five years old?	☐	☐
4. Does your family make a lot of short runs in the car which could be avoided?	☐	☐
5. Has the air-conditioning system not been checked since the car was bought?	☐	☐
6. Do the drivers in your family drive at high speeds and rev the engine impatiently when stuck in traffic jams?	☐	☐
7. Do your parents leave the car's engine running while you are grabbing your bags and piling into the car in the morning?	☐	☐
8. Do your parents forget to get the car serviced regularly?	☐	☐
9. Has it been over a week since your parents checked the pressure in their tyres?	☐	☐
10. Is your car boot full of lots of unnecessary stuff – like dad's golf clubs, deckchairs, kit bags, and so on?	☐	☐

No.77: Slow Down, You're Driving Too Fast

A car moving at very slow or very high speeds burns more petrol than one travelling at the recommended speed limit, because the engine works most efficiently at the recommended speed. So it's up to you to stop any member of your family crawling along or roaring away – stick to the limit.

Explain that driving 8 km per hour (5 miles per hour) below the speed limit over an 13 km (8 miles) journey will save 250 kg (550 lb) of CO_2 a year.

After all, what's the hurry?

No.78: Car Wash

Don't let your parents take the car to the automatic car wash. It uses a huge amount of water, electricity and chemicals to do something that you could achieve with a bucket and sponge.

Maybe washing the car by hand could be the punishment you hand out to members of the family who commit any of the eco-crimes described in this book.

No.79: Get On Your Bike

Cycling is a 100% green way to travel. Apart from the resources used in its manufacture and disposal, a bike never again damages the planet. Oh, and it's a great way of getting lots of exercise.

If you don't have a bike, ask around to see if anyone has outgrown theirs, or check out a car-boot fair or eBay. Get a friend to check your bike is roadworthy before you ride it.

WHEELY USEFUL TIPS

• Always wear a helmet and suitable clothing. After dark use lights and wear reflective clothing.

• Learn traffic codes and rules, and take a cycling proficiency test.

• Never listen to music while cycling on roads.

• Don't ride on pavements.

Did you know that riding a bike at a reasonable speed burns 400 calories an hour? Driving a car for an hour burns only 58 calories.

No.80: Best Foot Forward

Walking is a 100% cheap, green, and clean way of travelling. Whenever possible, make it your family mission to walk rather than drive – on short journeys to school or the local shops.

If your parents need further persuading, remind them that they won't need to spend ten minutes looking for a parking place or pay to park the car.

The diagram below compares how many tonnes of CO_2 is produced in a year by a daily ten-mile journey when it is made in a car, in a bus, on a train and on foot.

CAR
0.75 tonnes

BUS
0.6 tonnes

TRAIN
0.3 tonnes

FOOT
zero tonnes

No.81: Keep On Track

Railways are the greenest form of mass transport we have. Measured per person per mile, a rail journey produces less than $1/6$ of the CO_2 emissions of travelling by car. Next time your family plans a holiday or an outing, take responsibility for the travel arrangements, and research how you can get there and back by train.

No.82: Ground A Plane

The number of flights filling our skies is constantly increasing, as air travel gets cheaper and easier. Here's a shocking fact – every day, two-and-a-half-million people fly through the airspace directly over metropolitan Paris.

Next time you hear a plane overhead, look up and see if you can spot a spreading white line left behind it in the sky. These lines are actually condensation trails (or 'contrails'), and they form when hot, humid air coming out of a jet engine mixes with the colder air of the atmosphere.

Contrails may look white, but you should think of them as the dirty marks left by high-flying planes – or 'jetprints'.

They can spread out and form jet-made cirrus clouds. Unlike low-altitude clouds (which are thick and block sunlight), cirrus clouds let sunlight pass through them, but trap heat coming up from Earth. In short, contrails are contributing to the dangerous warming of our planet.

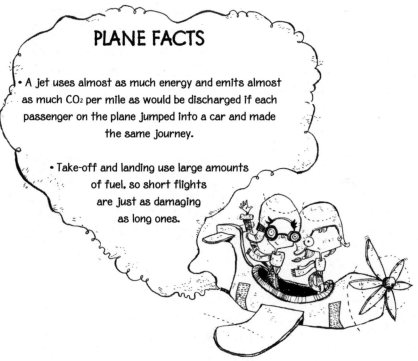

PLANE FACTS

• A jet uses almost as much energy and emits almost as much CO_2 per mile as would be discharged if each passenger on the plane jumped into a car and made the same journey.

• Take-off and landing use large amounts of fuel, so short flights are just as damaging as long ones.

OVER TO YOU

• Discuss with your family which flights you can avoid. It's great to go off on adventures abroad, but it's not great for our polluted atmosphere. If your family is planning a holiday this year, why not vote for taking one in the country you live? You could go camping, mountain biking, climbing, canoeing, horse riding – or stay on a farm.

No.83: Dirty Footprints

Every time we do something that results in greenhouse gases such as CO_2 being released into the air, we are making the world a dirtier, more polluted place to live. We are leaving filthy 'carbon footprints' all over the planet. Find out below what a carbon footprint is.

Carbon Footprint
A carbon footprint is a measure of the damaging effect that human activities have on the planet in terms of the amount of greenhouse gases these activities produce. Carbon footprints are measured in units of CO_2.

CARBON FOOTPRINT

Your family's carbon footprint is a measure of the CO_2 emissions caused by the time you spend watching television, heating your home or playing video games, the car journeys you make, the flights you take and the amount of stuff you buy and the things you don't recycle.

Your ecological footprint is the amount of land it takes to support you. This includes not only the land needed to grow all the food you eat, but the water you drink, the materials used to make the things you buy, and the space needed to bury your rubbish. The average person's annual ecological footprint is 6 acres (2.4 hectares) of land. This is about 20% bigger than it should be. For this planet to have room for all of us to live well, we all need to be a lot less greedy in the future. In developed countries, most of us are taking more than our fair share.

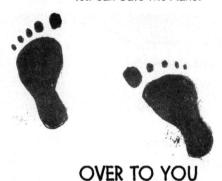

OVER TO YOU

• Calculate your household's carbon footprint – as this will really bring home to the members of your family how important it is to save energy.
Set a goal for how much you are going to reduce this footprint by in one year's time.

There are websites that will calculate your footprint for you.
Try www.carbonfootprint.com/calculator.html
or www.carboncalculator.co.uk

You will be asked questions like how many people live in your household, how you travel, and what the annual energy bills for your house are. Gather this information before you use the calculators.

No.84: Investigate Carbon Offsetting

If our planet is going to survive, it is important that we all make an effort to cut down or balance out, the amount of greenhouse gases we are releasing into the atmosphere. One way to do this is by 'carbon offsetting'.

Carbon Offsetting

Carbon offsetting is a method people and companies use to counteract the greenhouse gas emissions their activities produce. They pay organisations either to take greenhouse gases out of the atmosphere or to reduce emissions in another part of the world. Carbon offsetting reduces the effect of greenhouse gas emissions with the aim of combating global warming.

CARBON OFFSETTING

Carbon offsetting organisations counteract greenhouse gases in different ways. Some use the money you give them to plant trees that will absorb CO_2 and 'breathe out' oxygen. Other organisations will invest the money you give them in research and developing methods of producing renewable energy.

Make it your job to investigate carbon offsetting organisations on the Web and encourage your family to offset emissions. But remember, REDUCING your carbon emissions in the first place is always BETTER than offsetting them.

No.85: Offset Your Own Carbon

How about carbon offsetting your own pollution? It's not as easy as you think. For example, if you were driven to school this morning, how could you offset it? Choose from the offsetting options suggested opposite.

Carbon Crime:

DROVE TO SCHOOL TODAY.

Offsetting Options:

CATCH THE BUS HOME.

HAVE A COLD SANDWICH FOR DINNER.

TURN OFF THE HEATING.

DO YOUR HOMEWORK BY DAYLIGHT, NOT ELECTRIC LIGHT.

WALK TO SCHOOL TOMORROW.

PLANT A TREE.

SWITCH OFF THE TV OR COMPUTER FOR AN EVENING.

USE ONLY ONE SHEET OF LOO PAPER. (A TREE SAVED = MORE CARBON DIOXIDE ABSORBED FROM THE AIR.)

Some of these are a bit silly, but the idea is that you get your carbon-life balanced out. So, if you want a hot bath today, take a short shower for the rest of the week. If you realise you left a light on all night, tomorrow put on a jump instead of turning up the heating. If you bought someth new today, make sure you recycle something tom

Chapter Six

Save All Species

This section looks at the plants and animals that inhabit the planet. They need saving, too.

Right now, more species of animals and insects are disappearing from our planet than ever before. Some scientists think as many as a million species of plants and animals are currently in danger of becoming extinct. Most of them will disappear as a result of the things human beings do.

Make sure you are not one of the planet's most wanted eco-criminals.

No.86: Don't Be A Travelling Troublemaker

Some kinds of tourism are harming our planet. Imagine you found an undiscovered place with beautiful sandy beaches, wonderful fish in the sea, and forests filled with animals, birds and insects. When you got home you told all your friends about this place and they decided to visit it.

Here are some environmental consequences that might happen within five years of you sharing your secret:

Year One: There are camps all over the beach, and a property developer has plans to build a 5-star hotel.

Year Two: Much of the forest has been cut down to make room for a golf course and tennis courts.

Year Three: When the hotel is full of guests there won't be enough food available locally to feed everyone. Many products will have to be transported in, using lots of fuel.

Year Four: The daily boat trips to and from the island are disturbing the fish and polluting the water, and the local coral reef has also been damaged by pleasure-cruise trips and by careless divers.

Year Five: The hotel has created a lot of rubbish and sewage. Some of it is being taken away, but some of it is now being burnt or buried on the island, or even dumped into the sea . . .

. . . oops.

So you see how you may need to consider avoiding holidays to exotic, unspoilt locations that are expensive not only for your family, but also for the planet.

No.87: Sponsor A Rainforest

Do you want to know a really, really scary fact? Without rainforests, all life on this planet may become unsustainable. Due to tree clearance and logging, rainforests are being destroyed at a truly horrifying rate – about the equivalent of two football fields every second.

Almost half of Earth's rainforests are already gone for good, and at this rate, by 2060, there will be none remaining.

Get everyone you know to sponsor a rainforest. Check out the Web for organisations that are trying to save rainforests. If your friends ask why they should get involved, tell them to check out the facts on the following page.

FOREST FACTS

• Tropical rainforests are the single greatest producer of the air that we breathe.

• Tropical rainforests absorb huge quantities of poisonous CO_2. In doing so, they stabilise the world's climate.

• The clearing and burning of our rainforests accounts for up to 25% of the greenhouse gases produced by humans.

• Rainforests influence weather by controlling rainfall and the evaporation of water from soil.

• Rainforests are home not only to indigenous tribespeople, but also to two-thirds of all the living species on the planet (about 50 to 70 million different life forms).

• Over one third of the medicines in the developed world have ingredients which derive from rainforest plants. For example, the rosy periwinkle of Madagascar is used to treat childhood leukemia. These ingredients would disappear if the rainforests were destroyed.

No.88: Don't Pick Wild Plants

Many wild flowers and plants have disappeared, or are in danger of disappearing. One of the main causes of this is the clearing of woodlands, hedgerows and forests to make way for agriculture. However, the picking of wild flowers is also a huge problem. Many plants, from orchids to moss, are now protected, because in the past people have picked too many and have dramatically reduced their numbers.

Never pick wild plants and flowers when you are out walking and tell off any member of your family who does.

No.89: Beware Of Holiday Souvenirs

Tourist souvenirs are threatening some of our most endangered plants and animals. More than 800 species of animals and plants are currently banned from international trade and many thousands are subject to tight controls.

So think twice before you buy your souvenir. What's more, you might be breaking the law if you buy them.

MY FORBIDDEN SOUVENIR LIST

• Cacti

• Caviar

• Coral, ivory or tortoise shell (often made into jewellery)

• Crocodile, snake or lizard skins (this includes
shoes, belts and watch straps)

• Plants, such as orchids (these could be rare and
may well be unsuited to growing where you live)

• Leopard, tiger or seal skins (sometimes
made into key rings or purses)

• Live birds, insects, animals

• Sea shells (giant clam shells and conches are certainly
a no go, but all types are best left in the sea)

No.90: Don't Buy Fur

If you buy anything that looks furry, check that it is man-made. The fur of many animals — including cats and dogs — currently ends up in pom-poms, fur-lined boots, fur-trimmed coats and gloves, and toys such as animal figurines.

Be aware too that labels can be misleading. That item made with fur, described as imitation, may not be fake after all. Don't chance it, don't buy it.

NOT FURRY NICE FACTS

• An estimated two million cats and dogs are killed each year in China. Many are skinned alive.

• Over 30 million animals a year are killed on fur farms.

• It requires the fur of 100 chinchillas to make one human-sized fur coat.

• In spite of a government ban on the killing of young seals and pups, 268,921 seals were killed off the coast of Canada in 1996.

No:91: Adopt An Animal

Some of our favourite animals are in danger of becoming extinct – because of us. Rare animals are killed for their skins, tusks and horns, and even for sport . . . gross! Wildlife organisations are doing as much as they can to protect these animals, but your help is needed.

OVER TO YOU

• For a small amount of money each month, you could help to save a panda, a gorilla, an elephant or a rhinoceros – and you won't even have to feed or clean it! If you can't afford this yourself, ask if you can adopt an animal for your birthday or a Christmas present.

Once you have chosen your animal and arranged to pay your donation, you should expect to receive an adoption certificate and information all about YOUR animal.

No.92: Go To The Zoo

Zoos and safari parks are committed to saving endangered species, and your entrance fee alone will help to keep an animal safe and fed.

Make sure you support your local zoo or wildlife park by paying it a visit. Find out about the animals looked after and bred there. Remember they are not just there for you to look at, however. They are there because we have destroyed their homes and habitats, and have hunted others near to extinction. Without your help, many of our favourite animals will no longer be seen anywhere on this earth.

No.93: Tackle A Fisherman

Many waterfowl die because they swallow lead fishing weights with their food. Lead is a very poisonous substance. A short time ago, fishermen were banned from using it which has reduced the problem. However, waterbirds such as swans are also at risk from carelessly discarded fish hooks and lengths of nylon fishing line – both can cause our beautiful waterbirds to suffer painful deaths.

If you or anyone you know likes to fish, make sure you and they are respectful of waterfowl and other vulnerable wildlife.

No.94: Tune In To Tuna

Fishermen have known for a long time that tuna fish like to swim beneath groups of dolphins. As dolphins are easier to spot, fishermen often cast their nets around them to catch the tuna fish swimming below.

It is thought that in the last 50 years around seven million dolphins have drowned as a result of becoming tangled up in nets.

Dolphins are still being caught up in fishing nets today. The good news is that in 1990 the 'Dolphin-Safe' label was introduced to tins of tuna, promising that no dolphins had been harmed in catching the fish. So check the labelling on any tin of tuna that you buy. If you can't see the words 'Dolphin-Safe', leave it on the supermarket shelf.

No.95: Don't Swim With Dolphins

Many tourist destinations offer their guests the chance to swim with dolphins. It sounds like an amazing thing to do and a unique celebration of these amazing creatures.

Unfortunately the dolphins that tourists swim with are often originally located at sea and deliberately driven into rivers to make them easier to get to. Some weaker and smaller dolphins don't survive this treatment. It is unfair to dolphins that they are no longer allowed to live in their natural environment.

No.96: Throw Fish A Line

In the last 50 years, rapid advances in commercial fishing technology have had a devastating effect on the number of fish in the planet's seas. Here's why:

FISHY FACTS

- Huge factory boats can stay at sea for several weeks until they are full. They freeze and can the fish on board.

- The use of radar to locate fish and the use of vast fishing nets means that few fish manage to evade capture. Mesh sizes used in nets have got smaller, so young fish are caught before they have time to reproduce.

- Thousands of porpoises and dolphins are killed by mistake every year by salmon and tuna fishing.

- Overfishing also threatens animals that depend on fish for their diet. For example, in the Antarctic, fishing for krill (small, red shrimps) may threaten the whales that need to eat them.

OVER TO YOU

- Be aware of which types of fish are under threat and make sure that your family doesn't buy these fish for dinner. The less demand there is the fewer will be caught.

No.97: Save A Whale

The blue whale is the largest living animal. In the last century some species of whales, such as blue whales and humpbacks, were hunted almost to extinction.

Governments around the world finally intervened, and since 1986 commercial whaling has been banned. As a result whale populations are slowly recovering. Sadly some countries (including Japan, Iceland and Norway) have started whaling again.

OVER TO YOU

• Why not ask your parents for a family trip to go whale watching? The organisation Greenpeace has made a pledge that states that when Icelandic waters are a home for whales and not a hunting ground, people will promise to come to see them. The idea is that more money can be raised from tourism than from killing whales.

133

Chapter Seven
Spread The Word

By now you should be well on the way to making your home a greener, cleaner place. However, it is very important that everyone you know makes the same effort.

Now you need to tell other people about all the things *they* can do to make a difference.

No.98: Round Up Some Eco-warriors

Word of mouth is the best way to change the world. Tell everyone at school what you have found out about energy saving and recycling. Discuss with them ways your school can reduce waste, recycle things and protect the environment.

Why not set up an ecology club and put out a newsletter telling people about the green projects you are working on?

Share ideas of how to go green with people by including information on your own website or MySpace page.

No.99: Bigger Is Better

Saving the planet is a lot of work for one person. Make sure you recycle this book by giving it to all your friends and family. Alternatively, sit them down and talk about the information you have read in this book and what can be done to help the planet. Tell them to spread the word, too. Together you can make a bigger difference.

No.100: Make A Friend Across The Globe

There are over 6,500,000,000 people on Earth, so there are plenty of new friends to be made and converted to your green cause. Let's face it, our planet needs all the friends it can get.

See if your school can correspond with a school somewhere else in the world. You could e-mail the pupils there. Find out what life is like in their country. What sort of things do they do to help the planet? Exchange ideas and plans. Remember, together you can save the world.

No.101: Sign On The Dotted Line

All that's left for you to do is to sign the planet pledge below and act on all the things you have read about in this book. Copy out the pledge and get all the members of your family to read the book and sign it, too.

MY PLEDGE TO THE PLANET

I promise faithfully to try to remember
all the things that I have read in this book and to
remember to do them.

I will not be responsible for destroying the planet's
future by doing things that make my life easier today.

Signed by ....

Witnessed by ....

MY FAMILY'S PLEDGE TO THE PLANET

We promise faithfully to try to remember
all the things that we have read in this book and to
remember to do them.

We will not be responsible for destroying the planet's
future by doing things that make our lives easier today.

Signed by ....

Signed by ....

Signed by ....

Signed by ....

Witnessed by ....

Useful Websites

Here are some great green websites to check out.

Environment Agency
www.environment-agency.gov.uk

Recycle City
www.epa.gov/recyclecity

Enviornmental Kids Club
www.epa.gov/kids/

Atmosphere, Climate & Environment
www.ace.mmu.ac.uk/kids/

Tike The Penguin
tiki.oneworld.net

BBC Science and Nature
www.bbc.co.uk/sn

Young People's Trust For The Environment
www.yptenc.org.uk

Greenpeace
www.greenpeace.org

Waste Online
www.wasteonline.org.uk

Collective Good Mobile Phone Recycling
www.collectivegood.com

The Carbon Trust
www.carbontrust.co.uk

Waste Watch
www.wastewatch.org.uk

Friends Of The Earth
www.foe.co.uk

Alliant Energy Kids
www.powerhousekids.com

Green Fibres
www.greenfibres.com

Carbon Footprint
www.carbonfootprint.com